DISCOVER
NEW YORK CITY

Dr. Maxwell Shimba

Printed by Shimba Publishing LLC
Printed in the United States of America

TABLE OF CONTENTS

INTRODUCTION

Exploring the Timeless Allure of New York City

New York City stands as one of the most iconic and influential metropolises in the world. Its allure is timeless, captivating people from all walks of life and every corner of the globe. This book, "New York Forever," embarks on a journey through the city's multifaceted essence, revealing the elements that make it an unparalleled urban wonder. From its rich historical tapestry to its dynamic cultural and economic landscapes, this volume delves deep into the heart of New York City, celebrating its past, present, and future.

The Allure of New York City

The allure of New York City is both palpable and enigmatic. It is a city that never sleeps, where dreams are born and aspirations are realized. Its energy is infectious, drawing millions to its bustling streets, towering skyscrapers, and vibrant neighborhoods. The promise of opportunity and the thrill of possibility are woven into the very fabric of the city.

Visitors and residents alike are enchanted by New York's unique blend of grit and glamour. The city's skyline, dominated by architectural marvels such as the Empire State Building and One World Trade Center, is a testament to human ingenuity and ambition. Meanwhile, its streets pulse with the rhythms of everyday life, from the hustle and bustle of Wall Street to the artistic expressions found in the East Village.

Historical Significance

New York City's historical significance is profound. It has been a beacon of hope and a symbol of freedom for centuries. The city played a crucial role in the birth of the United States, serving as the first capital of the new nation. Landmarks like the Statue of Liberty and Ellis Island stand as enduring symbols of the American Dream, welcoming millions of immigrants who have shaped the city's diverse cultural landscape.

Throughout its history, New York City has been a hub of innovation and progress. It was here that the modern skyscraper was born, and where the subway system revolutionized urban transportation. The city has been at the forefront of cultural movements, from the Harlem Renaissance to the birth of hip-hop. Its theaters, museums, and institutions have influenced art, music, literature, and thought across the globe.

A Tapestry of Diversity

New York City's greatest strength lies in its diversity. It is a melting pot where people of all backgrounds and cultures come together, creating a rich mosaic of languages, traditions, and experiences. Each neighborhood has its own distinct character, from the vibrant streets of Chinatown to the artistic enclave of Greenwich Village. This diversity is not only celebrated but also integral to the city's identity.

The city's cultural fabric is woven with countless stories of resilience and triumph. Immigrant communities have preserved their heritage while contributing to the city's evolution. The food, festivals, and traditions of these communities offer a glimpse into the world, making New York a global city in every sense.

Captivating the World

New York City's influence extends far beyond its geographic boundaries. It is a global center for finance, fashion, media, and technology. Wall Street's financial markets set the pace for the global economy, while the fashion industry dictates trends worldwide. Media giants based in the city shape public opinion and culture on a massive scale. The tech sector, with its burgeoning Silicon Alley, drives innovation and entrepreneurship.

Yet, it is not only these industries that captivate the world. The city's cultural exports, from Broadway shows to groundbreaking art exhibitions, resonate with audiences everywhere. Its landmarks, such as Central Park, Times Square, and the Brooklyn Bridge, are etched into the collective imagination, symbolizing the spirit of New York.

A City of Endless Possibilities

New York City is a place of endless possibilities. It is where aspiring artists, entrepreneurs, and dreamers come to make their mark. The city's relentless pace and competitive spirit push individuals to reach new heights. Stories of success and reinvention are woven into the city's narrative, inspiring generations to believe that anything is possible.

The city's challenges, from economic inequality to environmental sustainability, are met with resilience and innovation. New Yorkers are known for their ability to adapt and thrive in the face of adversity. This spirit of determination and perseverance continues to drive the city forward, ensuring that it remains a beacon of hope and opportunity.

Conclusion

"New York Forever" is a tribute to this extraordinary city. Each chapter of this book explores different aspects of New York, from its economic powerhouse to its cultural and social fabric. Through this exploration, we aim to capture the essence of a city that has shaped history and continues to inspire the world.

As we embark on this journey, we invite you to experience the magic of New York City. Whether you are a lifelong resident, a frequent visitor, or someone who has yet to set foot in this metropolis, there is always something new to discover. New York's story is one of constant evolution, a testament to the enduring allure of a city that truly never sleeps.

Welcome to "New York Forever." Welcome to the heart of a city that captivates, inspires, and endures.

DR. MAXWELL SHIMBA

CHAPTER 01

THE ORIGINS OF NEW YORK

New York City, often referred to as the "Big Apple" or "The City That Never Sleeps," has a rich history that dates back over four centuries. The city's origins are deeply rooted in its strategic location, diverse population, and dynamic economy. Understanding New York's beginnings provides insight into how it evolved into one of the most influential cities in the world.

Early Beginnings: Lenape Land

Before European settlers arrived, the area now known as New York was inhabited by the Lenape, a Native American people who lived in a region they called Lenapehoking. The Lenape were primarily hunter-gatherers but also engaged in agriculture, cultivating crops such as corn, beans, and squash. They lived in small communities along the waterways and had a rich culture that included complex social structures, spiritual beliefs, and a deep connection to the land.

The Dutch Arrival: New Amsterdam

In 1609, English explorer Henry Hudson, sailing under the Dutch East India Company, arrived at the area while searching for a northwest passage to Asia. Hudson's exploration laid the groundwork for Dutch claims to the region. By 1624, the Dutch had established a permanent settlement on the southern tip of Manhattan Island, naming it New Amsterdam. The Dutch West India Company, which controlled the colony, encouraged settlement and trade.

New Amsterdam quickly became a thriving port due to its strategic location at the mouth of the Hudson River. The Dutch engaged in fur trading with the Native Americans and established a network of trading posts and settlements throughout the region. The colony's population grew with the arrival of settlers from various parts of Europe, creating a diverse and multicultural community.

The English Takeover: New York

In 1664, during the Second Anglo-Dutch War, the English captured New Amsterdam without a fight. The English renamed the city New York in honor of the Duke of York, who later became King James II. This change in power marked the beginning of English dominance in the region.

Under English rule, New York continued to grow as a center of commerce and trade. The city's harbor, one of the best natural harbors in the world, facilitated the import and export of goods, making New York a crucial link in the Atlantic trade routes. The population expanded rapidly, attracting immigrants from England, Scotland, Ireland, France, and other parts of Europe. This influx of people further enriched the city's cultural and economic landscape.

Colonial New York: A Melting Pot

By the early 18th century, New York had become one of the most important cities in the American colonies. Its population was a mix of different ethnicities and religions, including Dutch, English, French Huguenots, Jews, Africans, and Native Americans. This diversity was reflected in the city's architecture, culture, and social fabric.

Economically, New York prospered as a center of trade, finance, and industry. The city's merchants engaged in international trade, exporting goods such as furs, timber, and agricultural products while importing manufactured goods from Europe. The growth of commerce led to the development of banking and insurance industries, laying the foundation for New York's future as a global financial hub.

Revolutionary War and Independence

New York played a significant role in the American Revolution. In 1765, the Stamp Act Congress met in New York to protest British taxation, marking an early step toward colonial unity and resistance. During the war, the city was a major strategic objective due to its port and its position as a center of British military operations.

In 1776, George Washington and the Continental Army suffered a significant defeat in the Battle of Long Island, leading to the British occupation of New York City for most of the war. Despite this setback, New York's residents continued to support the revolutionary cause through espionage, smuggling, and other means.

When the war ended in 1783, New York emerged as a symbol of American resilience and independence. The city hosted the inauguration of George Washington as the first President of the United States in 1789, further cementing its place in the nation's history.

Post-Revolution Growth

After the Revolution, New York entered a period of rapid growth and transformation. The opening of the Erie Canal in 1825 connected the city to the Great Lakes and the Midwest, dramatically increasing trade and commerce. The canal made New York the primary gateway for goods entering and leaving the interior of the United States, fueling the city's economic expansion.

The 19th century saw New York become the nation's largest city and a global center for finance, industry, and culture. The arrival of millions of immigrants through Ellis

Island in the late 19th and early 20th centuries further diversified the city's population and contributed to its dynamic character.

The origins of New York City are a testament to the power of diversity, strategic location, and economic opportunity. From its beginnings as Lenape land to its transformation into New Amsterdam and then New York, the city has always been a melting pot of cultures and a hub of commerce. Understanding this history provides a foundation for appreciating the vibrant, ever-evolving metropolis that New York is today. As we delve deeper into the city's various aspects in subsequent chapters, the rich tapestry of its past will continue to inform and inspire.

CHAPTER 02

THE IMMIGRANT EXPERIENCE

New York City's story is, at its heart, a story of immigration. For centuries, people from all over the world have come to New York in search of a better life. Their experiences, struggles, and contributions have woven the intricate cultural fabric of the city, making it a true melting pot. This chapter explores the immigrant experience in New York City, from the waves of immigration in the 19th and 20th centuries to the modern-day arrivals that continue to shape the city's identity.

Ellis Island: Gateway to America

For millions of immigrants, Ellis Island was their first glimpse of America. Opened in 1892, Ellis Island served as the primary immigration station for the United States until 1954. Over 12 million immigrants passed through its doors, undergoing medical and legal inspections before being allowed to enter the country.

The experience at Ellis Island was often overwhelming. After long and arduous journeys across the Atlantic, immigrants were greeted by the imposing sight of the Statue of Liberty, a symbol of hope and freedom. Once at Ellis Island, they faced a rigorous screening process. Those who passed were allowed to continue their journey into America; those who did not were sent back to their countries of origin.

The stories of those who passed through Ellis Island are as diverse as the people themselves. Many immigrants faced significant challenges, including language barriers, cultural differences, and economic hardship. However, their determination and resilience enabled them to build new lives and contribute to the city's growth and development.

The Waves of Immigration

New York City experienced several major waves of immigration, each bringing different groups with unique cultural backgrounds and skills.

1. The First Wave (1820-1880): The first significant wave of immigrants came from Northern and Western Europe, primarily Ireland and Germany. The Irish fled the Great Famine of the 1840s, while many Germans sought to escape political unrest and economic hardship. These

immigrants settled in various neighborhoods, forming tight-knit communities that maintained their cultural heritage.

2. The Second Wave (1880-1920): The second wave brought immigrants from Southern and Eastern Europe, including Italians, Jews, Poles, and Russians. This period also saw the arrival of Asian immigrants, particularly Chinese laborers. These new arrivals settled in neighborhoods like Little Italy, the Lower East Side, and Chinatown, enriching the city's cultural diversity.

3. The Third Wave (1965-Present): The Immigration and Nationality Act of 1965 abolished the national origins quota system, leading to a surge in immigration from Latin America, Asia, and Africa. This wave included a significant number of immigrants from the Caribbean, Central America, South Asia, and East Asia. These groups have established vibrant communities in neighborhoods such as Jackson Heights, Flushing, and Washington Heights.

Challenges and Contributions

Immigrants have faced numerous challenges upon arriving in New York City. Language barriers, cultural differences, and economic difficulties often made the transition to life in America challenging. Many immigrants lived in overcrowded tenements in poor conditions, worked in low-paying jobs, and faced discrimination and prejudice.

Despite these challenges, immigrants have made significant contributions to New York City. They have played crucial roles in building the city's infrastructure, fueling its economy, and enriching its cultural landscape. Immigrant labor was essential in constructing iconic landmarks like the Brooklyn Bridge and the skyscrapers of Manhattan. Immigrants also established businesses, from small family-owned shops to large enterprises, contributing to the city's economic growth.

Culturally, immigrants have left an indelible mark on New York City. The city's cuisine, festivals, music, and arts reflect its diverse population. From the Italian-American Feast of San Gennaro in Little Italy to the vibrant celebrations of Chinese New Year in Chinatown, these cultural expressions have become integral parts of New York's identity.

Neighborhoods and Communities

New York City s neighborhoods are a testament to its rich immigrant history. Each neighborhood has its unique character, shaped by the people who have lived there and their cultural traditions.

1. Chinatown: One of the oldest and most famous immigrant neighborhoods, Chinatown is home to a large

Chinese population. It boasts a vibrant cultural scene with traditional restaurants, shops, temples, and festivals.

2. Little Italy: Originally populated by Italian immigrants, Little Italy is known for its authentic Italian restaurants, bakeries, and the annual Feast of San Gennaro. While the Italian population has decreased, the neighborhood retains its cultural heritage.

3. Harlem: Initially an African-American cultural hub during the Harlem Renaissance, Harlem has also seen an influx of West African and Caribbean immigrants. The neighborhood is famous for its music, particularly jazz, and cultural institutions like the Apollo Theater.

4. Jackson Heights: One of the most diverse neighborhoods in New York, Jackson Heights is home to immigrants from Latin America, South Asia, and East Asia. The neighborhood offers a wide array of international cuisines and cultural festivals.

5. Washington Heights: Known for its large Dominican population, Washington Heights is a vibrant community with Dominican restaurants, businesses, and cultural events.

Modern Immigration

Today, New York City continues to be a beacon for immigrants from around the world. Modern immigrants come from diverse regions, including Latin America, the Caribbean, Asia, and Africa. They bring with them their cultural traditions, languages, and aspirations, contributing to the ever-evolving mosaic of the city.

Organizations and community groups play a vital role in supporting new immigrants, providing services such as language classes, legal assistance, and job training. These efforts help immigrants integrate into the city's social and economic fabric while preserving their cultural identities.

The immigrant experience is central to the story of New York City. From the early settlers who established New Amsterdam to the modern-day arrivals who continue to shape the city's future, immigrants have been the lifeblood of New York. Their stories of hardship, resilience, and success reflect the broader American experience and underscore the city's enduring appeal as a place of opportunity and diversity. As we explore other facets of New York in the following chapters, the contributions of its immigrant population will remain a recurring and integral theme.

CHAPTER 03

THE SKYLINE OF DREAMS

New York City's skyline is one of the most recognizable in the world. It tells the story of architectural innovation, economic ambition, and the human drive to reach new heights. This chapter delves into the evolution of New York's skyline, highlighting the iconic buildings that define it and the visionaries who shaped the city's vertical expansion.

Early Architecture: Foundations of the Skyline

New York City's architectural journey began in the 17th century with modest Dutch and English colonial structures. These early buildings were functional and simplistic, made from wood and stone. As the city grew, the architectural style began to evolve, reflecting the influences of various immigrant groups and the city's increasing wealth.

By the mid-19th century, New York was experiencing rapid growth and industrialization. The introduction of cast iron allowed for the construction of taller and more elaborate buildings. The SoHo district, with its cast-iron facades, is a lasting example of this period. These structures, although not skyscrapers by modern standards, laid the groundwork for the city's architectural ambitions.

The Birth of the Skyscraper

The late 19th and early 20th centuries marked the beginning of the skyscraper era in New York City. Advances in steel construction, combined with the invention of the safety elevator by Elisha Otis in 1857, made it possible to build higher than ever before. This period saw the construction of some of the city's most iconic early skyscrapers.

1. The Flatiron Building (1902): Designed by Daniel Burnham, the Flatiron Building was one of the first skyscrapers to capture public imagination. Its distinctive triangular shape and Beaux-Arts style made it a beloved landmark.

2. The Woolworth Building (1913): Known as the "Cathedral of Commerce," the Woolworth Building was the tallest building in the world when it was completed. Designed by Cass Gilbert, its neo-Gothic architecture and intricate detailing symbolized the commercial power of New York.

3. The Chrysler Building (1930): An Art Deco masterpiece, the Chrysler Building briefly held the title of the

world's tallest building. Designed by William Van Alen, its stainless steel spire and ornate crown remain a testament to the exuberance of the Roaring Twenties.

4. The Empire State Building (1931): Completed during the Great Depression, the Empire State Building became an icon of hope and resilience. Designed by Shreve, Lamb & Harmon, it held the title of the world's tallest building for nearly 40 years. Its sleek, symmetrical design and observatory decks continue to attract millions of visitors annually.

The Modern Era: Mid-20th Century to Present

The mid-20th century saw a shift in architectural styles and the emergence of modernist principles. This period was marked by the construction of buildings that emphasized simplicity, functionality, and the use of new materials like glass and steel.

1. The Seagram Building (1958): Designed by Ludwig Mies van der Rohe and Philip Johnson, the Seagram Building is a prime example of International Style architecture. Its minimalist design, with a bronze and glass facade, set a new standard for corporate buildings.

2. The World Trade Center (1973): The twin towers of the World Trade Center, designed by Minoru Yamasaki, symbolized New York's role as a global financial hub. Their

tragic destruction in the 9/11 attacks marked a significant chapter in the city's history, leading to the redevelopment of the World Trade Center site.

3. One World Trade Center (2014): Also known as the Freedom Tower, One World Trade Center stands as a symbol of resilience and renewal. Designed by David Childs of Skidmore, Owings & Merrill, it is the tallest building in the Western Hemisphere, combining state-of-the-art technology with sustainable design.

Architectural Innovation and Sustainability

New York City continues to push the boundaries of architectural innovation and sustainability. Modern skyscrapers are designed not only for aesthetic appeal but also for environmental efficiency and resilience against natural disasters.

1. The Hearst Tower (2006): Designed by Norman Foster, the Hearst Tower is a model of sustainable design. It was the first skyscraper in New York to receive a LEED Gold certification. Its distinctive diagrid structure reduces the amount of steel needed and enhances structural stability.

2. The Bank of America Tower (2009): Designed by Cookfox Architects, this skyscraper incorporates numerous green technologies, including waterless urinals, a greywater

recycling system, and a high-performance glass facade that reduces heat gain.

3. Hudson Yards (2019): The Hudson Yards development is a massive project on Manhattan's West Side, featuring innovative architecture and sustainable design. The centerpiece, The Vessel, designed by Thomas Heatherwick, offers a unique interactive experience, while the surrounding skyscrapers include cutting-edge office spaces and residences.

The Visionaries: Architects and Developers

The transformation of New York's skyline has been driven by visionary architects and developers. Figures like Cass Gilbert, William Van Alen, Ludwig Mies van der Rohe, and more recently, David Childs and Norman Foster, have left their mark on the city. Their designs reflect not only the architectural trends of their times but also the aspirations and values of New York itself.

Developers like the Rockefeller family, who built Rockefeller Center, and Larry Silverstein, who played a crucial role in the redevelopment of the World Trade Center, have been instrumental in shaping the city's built environment. Their projects often involved overcoming significant financial, technical, and political challenges, underscoring the complex nature of urban development.

Cultural and Social Impact

The skyline of New York City is more than just a collection of buildings; it is a symbol of human achievement and aspiration. The city's skyscrapers are landmarks of architectural innovation, economic power, and cultural significance. They have been featured in countless films, television shows, and works of art, reinforcing New York's image as a global metropolis.

The skyline also reflects the social and economic dynamics of the city. The construction of skyscrapers has often been accompanied by debates over issues such as urban density, gentrification, and the displacement of communities. These discussions highlight the need to balance development with the preservation of the city's character and the well-being of its residents.

The skyline of New York City is a living testament to the city's history, ambition, and resilience. From the early colonial structures to the towering skyscrapers of today, each building tells a story of architectural innovation and human endeavor. As New York continues to grow and evolve, its skyline will undoubtedly change, but it will always remain a symbol of the city's enduring spirit and its place on the world stage.

In the following chapters, we will explore other aspects of New York that contribute to its unique character, from its vibrant cultural scene to its diverse neighborhoods. Each facet of the city adds to the rich tapestry that makes New York an unparalleled urban experience.

CHAPTER 04

THE HEARTBEAT OF THE CITY-CENTRAL PARK

Central Park is often referred to as the "lungs" of New York City, providing a vital green oasis in the midst of Manhattan's concrete jungle. Spanning 843 acres, Central Park is more than just a park; it is a cultural and social hub that plays a crucial role in the life of the city. This chapter explores the history, design, and impact of Central Park on New York City and its residents.

The Vision and Creation of Central Park

In the mid-19th century, New York City was rapidly expanding, and the need for a large public park became evident. The idea for Central Park was conceived as a response to the growing urbanization and the desire to provide a natural escape for the city's inhabitants. In 1853, the New York State Legislature set aside over 700 acres of land in the center of Manhattan for the creation of the park.

A design competition was held in 1857, and the winning entry was the "Greensward Plan," created by landscape architects Frederick Law Olmsted and Calvert Vaux. Their vision for Central Park was inspired by the pastoral landscapes of England and sought to create a harmonious balance between nature and urban life. Construction began in 1858 and continued for over 15 years, involving the labor of thousands of workers who transformed the rocky, swampy terrain into a verdant paradise.

Design and Features

Olmsted and Vaux's design for Central Park incorporated various elements intended to provide diverse recreational opportunities and scenic beauty. The park's design includes meadows, woodlands, water bodies, and carefully crafted vistas. Key features of Central Park include:

1. The Mall and Literary Walk: A broad promenade lined with American elms, leading to a collection of statues honoring famous writers. This area is popular for leisurely strolls and gatherings.

2. Bethesda Terrace and Fountain: Considered the heart of Central Park, Bethesda Terrace features intricate carvings and offers stunning views of the lake and surrounding landscapes. The Bethesda Fountain, topped with

the Angel of the Waters statue, is one of the most iconic spots in the park.

3. The Great Lawn: An expansive open area used for picnics, sports, and concerts. It is a popular spot for sunbathing and outdoor activities.

4. The Ramble: A wooded area with winding paths, streams, and a diverse array of plant and bird species. It offers a more natural, secluded experience within the park.

5. The Reservoir: Officially named the Jacqueline Kennedy Onassis Reservoir, this large water body is encircled by a running track and provides scenic views of the city skyline.

6. Strawberry Fields: A tribute to John Lennon, this peaceful area features the "Imagine" mosaic and is a place of reflection and remembrance.

7. Belvedere Castle: A miniature castle offering panoramic views of the park and the city. It houses a visitor center and a weather station.

Cultural and Recreational Activities

Central Park is not just a place for passive enjoyment of nature; it is a vibrant space for a wide range of cultural and recreational activities. The park hosts numerous events and performances throughout the year, including:

1. SummerStage: An annual festival featuring free concerts, dance performances, and theatrical productions in various genres, attracting both locals and tourists.

2. Shakespeare in the Park: A beloved tradition since 1962, the Public Theater presents free productions of Shakespeare's plays at the Delacorte Theater in Central Park.

3. Central Park Zoo: Located in the southeast corner of the park, the zoo features a variety of animals and educational programs, making it a popular destination for families.

4. Sports and Fitness: Central Park offers facilities for a variety of sports, including baseball fields, tennis courts, and ice skating rinks. The park is also a haven for runners, cyclists, and walkers, with miles of paths and trails.

5. Boating and Rowing: The park's lakes and ponds provide opportunities for boating and rowing, offering a serene escape from the hustle and bustle of the city.

6. Holiday Events: Central Park is a hub of activity during the holiday season, with events like the annual Christmas tree lighting at the Charles A. Dana Discovery Center and the New Year's Eve Midnight Run.

Impact on New York City

Central Park has had a profound impact on the development and character of New York City. Its creation set a precedent for urban park design and inspired the establishment of other parks across the United States. The park's presence has also influenced real estate values, with properties adjacent to Central Park commanding some of the highest prices in the city.

Beyond its economic impact, Central Park plays a crucial role in the social and environmental health of New York. It provides a space for community interaction, relaxation, and physical activity, contributing to the well-being of the city's residents. The park's green spaces help mitigate the urban heat island effect, improve air quality, and provide habitat for wildlife.

Challenges and Preservation Efforts

Maintaining Central Park's beauty and accessibility requires ongoing effort and investment. Over the years, the park has faced challenges, including periods of neglect and financial difficulties. In the 1970s and 1980s, budget cuts and declining conditions led to widespread deterioration and safety concerns.

In response, the Central Park Conservancy was established in 1980 as a private nonprofit organization dedicated to the restoration and maintenance of the park. The Conservancy works in partnership with the City of New York to manage Central Park, raising funds, organizing volunteer efforts, and implementing preservation projects. Their work has been instrumental in revitalizing the park and ensuring its sustainability for future generations.

Central Park is a cherished treasure in the heart of New York City, offering a respite from urban life and a space for recreation, culture, and community. Its history, design, and impact illustrate the importance of green spaces in urban environments and the enduring value of visionary planning and stewardship. As we continue to explore New York in the following chapters, the role of Central Park will remain a central theme, reflecting the city's commitment to preserving its natural and cultural heritage.

Next, we will delve into the vibrant arts and cultural scene of New York City, examining how the city has become a global hub for creativity and innovation. From Broadway to the Metropolitan Museum of Art, New York's cultural institutions and artistic communities play a pivotal role in shaping its identity and attracting millions of visitors from around the world.

CHAPTER 05

THE CULTURAL MELTING POT

New York City is renowned for its rich and diverse cultural scene, a vibrant tapestry woven from the contributions of countless artists, performers, and visionaries. This chapter explores how the city has become a global hub for arts and culture, examining key institutions, movements, and events that have shaped its cultural landscape.

Broadway and Theater District

Broadway is synonymous with the pinnacle of theatrical performance. Located in the heart of Manhattan, the Broadway Theater District is home to over 40 professional theaters, attracting millions of theatergoers each year.

1. Historical Development: Broadway's origins date back to the early 19th century when theaters began to proliferate along Broadway and in nearby areas. By the early

20th century, Broadway had established itself as the premier destination for high-quality theater.

2. Iconic Productions: From classic musicals like The Phantom of the Opera and Les Misérables to contemporary hits like Hamilton and Dear Evan Hansen, Broadway productions have set the standard for theatrical excellence. The impact of these shows extends far beyond New York, with many productions touring globally and influencing the wider performing arts world.

3. Tony Awards: The annual Tony Awards, named after actress Antoinette Perry, celebrate the best of Broadway theater. Winning a Tony is considered one of the highest honors in the industry, recognizing outstanding achievements in acting, directing, and production.

Museums and Galleries

New York City boasts some of the most prestigious museums and galleries in the world, offering a wide range of artistic and historical experiences.

1. The Metropolitan Museum of Art: Known as The Met, this institution is the largest art museum in the United States. It houses over two million works of art spanning 5,000 years, from ancient artifacts to contemporary masterpieces. The Met's annual Costume Institute Gala, or Met Gala, is a

major cultural event that draws celebrities and fashion icons from around the globe.

2. The Museum of Modern Art (MoMA): MoMA is one of the world's leading institutions dedicated to modern and contemporary art. Its collection includes works by Picasso, Van Gogh, Warhol, and many other influential artists. MoMA's exhibitions and programs are pivotal in promoting innovative artistic expressions.

3. The Solomon R. Guggenheim Museum: Designed by renowned architect Frank Lloyd Wright, the Guggenheim is an architectural marvel as well as a premier venue for modern art. Its spiral design provides a unique experience for visitors, showcasing exhibitions that challenge conventional artistic norms.

4. The American Museum of Natural History: Located on the Upper West Side, this museum is a treasure trove of natural history, anthropology, and science. It features impressive exhibits like the dinosaur fossils, the Hall of Ocean Life, and the Hayden Planetarium.

Music and Performing Arts

New York City's music scene is as diverse as its population, encompassing a wide range of genres and styles.

1. Carnegie Hall: Since its opening in 1891, Carnegie Hall has been one of the most prestigious concert venues in

the world. It hosts performances by leading orchestras, soloists, and ensembles across classical, jazz, and contemporary music.

2. The Apollo Theater: Located in Harlem, the Apollo Theater is a legendary venue that has played a crucial role in the careers of many African American artists, including Ella Fitzgerald, James Brown, and Michael Jackson. The Apollo's Amateur Night continues to be a platform for emerging talent.

3. Jazz at Lincoln Center: Dedicated to preserving and promoting jazz, this organization offers performances, educational programs, and archives that celebrate this quintessentially American art form. Its flagship venue, the Frederick P. Rose Hall, hosts concerts by some of the world's finest jazz musicians.

4. The New York Philharmonic: As the oldest symphony orchestra in the United States, the New York Philharmonic has a storied history of exceptional performances. Its home, David Geffen Hall at Lincoln Center, is a focal point for classical music enthusiasts.

Literature and Libraries

New York City has long been a haven for writers, poets, and literary enthusiasts.

1. The New York Public Library: With its iconic main branch on Fifth Avenue, the New York Public Library (NYPL) is one of the largest public library systems in the world. It offers extensive collections, research facilities, and public programs that foster a love of reading and learning.

2. The Strand Bookstore: An independent bookstore founded in 1927, the Strand is famous for its "18 miles of books." It is a beloved institution among New Yorkers and visitors alike, offering a vast selection of new, used, and rare books.

3. Literary Movements: New York has been the birthplace of several influential literary movements, including the Harlem Renaissance in the 1920s and the Beat Generation in the 1950s. Writers such as Langston Hughes, Jack Kerouac, and Allen Ginsberg found inspiration in the city's vibrant cultural scene.

Festivals and Cultural Events

New York City hosts numerous festivals and cultural events throughout the year, celebrating its diverse communities and artistic achievements.

1. Tribeca Film Festival: Founded by Robert De Niro, Jane Rosenthal, and Craig Hatkoff in 2002, the Tribeca Film Festival showcases a wide array of independent films, documentaries, and international cinema. It has become a

significant platform for filmmakers and a major event in the city's cultural calendar.

2. New York Fashion Week: Twice a year, New York Fashion Week brings designers, models, and fashion enthusiasts from around the world to the city. The event showcases the latest trends and collections, reinforcing New York's status as a global fashion capital.

3. Macy's Thanksgiving Day Parade: This iconic parade, featuring giant balloons, floats, and performances, has been a beloved Thanksgiving tradition since 1924. It attracts millions of spectators along its route and millions more who watch it on television.

4. Cultural Festivals: New York City's neighborhoods celebrate their heritage with various cultural festivals, such as the Puerto Rican Day Parade, the Chinese New Year Parade, and the West Indian American Day Carnival. These events highlight the city's multicultural identity and offer vibrant displays of music, dance, and cuisine.

The Cultural Impact

The cultural richness of New York City has a profound impact on its residents and the world at large. The city's arts and culture scene fosters creativity, innovation, and a sense of community. It attracts millions of visitors each year, contributing significantly to the local economy and reinforcing New York's reputation as a global cultural capital.

The city's cultural institutions and events also play a vital role in education and social cohesion. They provide opportunities for learning, engagement, and expression, helping to bridge gaps between different communities and generations.

New York City's cultural scene is a dynamic and integral part of its identity. From Broadway theaters and world-class museums to vibrant music venues and literary landmarks, the city's cultural offerings are as diverse as its population. As we continue our exploration of New York, we will delve into its neighborhoods and communities, examining how the city's unique blend of cultures and traditions shapes the everyday lives of its residents and contributes to its enduring allure.

In the next chapter, we will explore the economic engine of New York City, focusing on its role as a global financial center and the diverse industries that drive its economy. We will look at the historical development of Wall Street, the impact of various economic booms and busts, and the city's ongoing efforts to maintain its position as a leading economic powerhouse.

CHAPTER 06

THE ECONOMIC ENGINE – WALL STREET AND BEYOND

New York City is often described as the financial capital of the world, and Wall Street is at the heart of this reputation. This chapter explores the historical development, key institutions, and current dynamics of New York's financial sector, as well as its broader economic landscape, encompassing diverse industries that contribute to the city's economic vitality.

The Rise of Wall Street

Wall Street's origins date back to the 17th century when Dutch settlers established a trading post on the southern tip of Manhattan. Over time, it evolved into a center for trade and finance, with the Buttonwood Agreement of 1792 marking a significant milestone. Signed by 24 stockbrokers under a buttonwood tree, this agreement laid the foundation for what would become the New York Stock Exchange (NYSE).

1. New York Stock Exchange (NYSE): The NYSE, located at 11 Wall Street, is the largest stock exchange in the world by market capitalization. It has been a symbol of American capitalism and economic power, facilitating the trading of securities and serving as a barometer for global financial markets.

2. The Crash of 1929: The stock market crash of 1929, known as Black Tuesday, triggered the Great Depression and highlighted the risks of speculative investing. This event led to significant regulatory changes, including the creation of the Securities and Exchange Commission (SEC) to oversee the securities industry.

3. Financial Deregulation and the 2008 Crisis: The late 20th and early 21st centuries saw periods of financial deregulation, which contributed to economic booms and busts. The 2008 financial crisis, precipitated by the collapse of major financial institutions and the subprime mortgage market, had profound effects on the global economy and led to calls for stricter oversight and reform.

Key Financial Institutions

1. Investment Banks: Major investment banks such as Goldman Sachs, Morgan Stanley, and JPMorgan Chase have

their headquarters in New York City. These institutions play a critical role in underwriting securities, facilitating mergers and acquisitions, and providing financial advisory services.

2. Federal Reserve Bank of New York: As one of the 12 regional Reserve Banks in the Federal Reserve System, the Federal Reserve Bank of New York conducts monetary policy, supervises and regulates financial institutions, and provides financial services to the U.S. government and other central banks.

3. Insurance Companies: New York City is home to some of the world's largest insurance companies, including MetLife and AIG. These firms offer a wide range of insurance products and services, from life insurance to property and casualty coverage.

4. Hedge Funds and Private Equity: The city is a hub for hedge funds and private equity firms, which manage substantial assets and invest in a variety of financial instruments and businesses. These entities contribute to the dynamism and complexity of the financial markets.

The Broader Economic Landscape

While finance is a cornerstone of New York City's economy, the city boasts a diverse range of industries that drive economic growth and employment.

1. Real Estate: The real estate sector is one of the largest and most influential in New York City. Iconic skyscrapers, luxury residential buildings, and commercial properties contribute to the city's distinctive skyline and economic vitality. Real estate development and transactions are significant economic activities, with neighborhoods constantly evolving to meet the demands of residents and businesses.

2. Technology: Known as "Silicon Alley," New York City's tech sector has experienced rapid growth, with a focus on areas such as fintech, media, and e-commerce. Major tech companies, including Google, Facebook, and Amazon, have established substantial presences in the city, creating jobs and fostering innovation.

3. Media and Entertainment: New York is a global media capital, home to major television networks, film studios, publishing houses, and advertising agencies. The city's media industry produces influential content that reaches audiences worldwide, contributing to its cultural and economic impact.

4. Tourism and Hospitality: Tourism is a critical component of New York City's economy, attracting millions of visitors annually. Iconic landmarks such as the Statue of Liberty, Times Square, and the Empire State Building draw

tourists from around the globe. The hospitality industry, including hotels, restaurants, and entertainment venues, thrives on the steady influx of visitors.

5. Healthcare and Education: The city is a center for healthcare and education, with world-renowned hospitals and universities. Institutions like New York -Presbyterian Hospital, Mount Sinai, Columbia University, and New York University (NYU) not only provide essential services and education but also drive research and innovation in their respective fields.

Economic Challenges and Resilience

New York City's economy has faced numerous challenges, including economic downturns, natural disasters, and public health crises. The COVID-19 pandemic, for instance, had a profound impact on the city's economy, leading to job losses, business closures, and shifts in work and lifestyle patterns.

1. Economic Inequality: Despite its wealth and economic power, New York City grapples with significant economic inequality. High living costs, housing affordability, and wage disparities are persistent issues that affect many residents.

2. Economic Recovery and Adaptation: The city's resilience is evident in its ability to adapt and recover from

economic setbacks. Efforts to revitalize neighborhoods, support small businesses, and invest in infrastructure are ongoing. The city's recovery strategies often focus on fostering innovation, improving public services, and enhancing the quality of life for all its residents.

3. Sustainability and Climate Change: As a coastal city, New York faces challenges related to climate change and environmental sustainability. Initiatives to improve energy efficiency, reduce greenhouse gas emissions, and enhance resilience to extreme weather events are critical for the city's long-term economic and environmental health.

New York City's economic engine is a complex and dynamic system, driven by the interplay of finance, real estate, technology, media, tourism, healthcare, and education. Wall Street remains a symbol of the city's financial might, but it is the diversity of industries and the resilience of its people that truly sustain New York's economic vitality.

As we continue our journey through New York, we will next explore the city's neighborhoods and communities, delving into the unique character and history of areas such as Harlem, Greenwich Village, and Brooklyn. These neighborhoods are the lifeblood of the city, each contributing its own flavor to the rich tapestry that makes New York an ever-evolving, ever-fascinating metropolis.

CHAPTER 07

NEIGHBORHOODS AND COMMUNITIES – THE HEART OF THE CITY

New York City's neighborhoods are the heart and soul of the metropolis, each with its unique character, history, and culture. This chapter delves into some of the most iconic neighborhoods, exploring their origins, key landmarks, and the vibrant communities that call them home.

Harlem

Harlem is one of the most famous neighborhoods in New York City, known for its rich cultural heritage and pivotal role in African American history.

1. Historical Background: Harlem's history dates back to the Dutch settlement in the 17th century, but it gained prominence in the early 20th century as a major African American cultural and intellectual hub. The Harlem

Renaissance, a flourishing of black culture, art, literature, and music, took place during the 1920s and 1930s.

2. Cultural Landmarks: Key landmarks include the Apollo Theater, a historic venue that launched the careers of many legendary artists; the Studio Museum, which focuses on African American art; and the Schomburg Center for Research in Black Culture, a leading research library.

3. Community and Lifestyle: Harlem remains a vibrant community with a strong sense of identity. It hosts numerous cultural festivals, parades, and events that celebrate its heritage. The neighborhood is also known for its soul food restaurants, jazz clubs, and gospel choirs.

Greenwich Village

Greenwich Village, often simply called "The Village," is renowned for its bohemian culture, artistic community, and progressive history.

1. Historical Background: The Village became a magnet for artists, writers, and intellectuals in the late 19th and early 20th centuries. It was a center for the Beat Generation in the 1950s and the counterculture movement of the 1960s.

2. Cultural Landmarks: Key sites include Washington Square Park, a vibrant public space; the Stonewall Inn, the birthplace of the modern LGBTQ+ rights movement; and

the White Horse Tavern, a historic bar frequented by literary figures like Dylan Thomas and Jack Kerouac.

3. Community and Lifestyle: Greenwich Village is known for its charming streets, historic brownstones, and eclectic mix of shops, cafes, and theaters. The neighborhood continues to attract creative individuals and remains a bastion of progressive thought and cultural innovation.

Brooklyn

Brooklyn, the most populous borough of New York City, has a diverse array of neighborhoods, each with its own distinct character.

1. Williamsburg: Once an industrial area, Williamsburg has transformed into a trendy neighborhood known for its hipster culture, art scene, and vibrant nightlife. It features a mix of historic buildings and new developments, with popular attractions like the Brooklyn Brewery and the Smorgasburg food market.

2. DUMBO: Short for "Down Under the Manhattan Bridge Overpass," DUMBO is a former industrial district turned upscale neighborhood. It offers stunning views of the Manhattan skyline, art galleries, and the popular Brooklyn Bridge Park.

3. Bedford-Stuyvesant: Commonly known as Bed-Stuy, this neighborhood has a rich African American history

and is famous for its beautiful brownstones. It has seen significant revitalization in recent years, with new businesses and cultural institutions emerging alongside long-standing community traditions.

4. Coney Island: Coney Island is synonymous with seaside amusement. Its historic boardwalk, amusement park, and the annual Mermaid Parade are beloved by locals and tourists alike. The neighborhood is also home to the New York Aquarium.

The Bronx

The Bronx, the northernmost borough, is known for its cultural diversity, green spaces, and significant contributions to music and sports.

1. Yankee Stadium: Home to the New York Yankees, Yankee Stadium is a major landmark and a symbol of the Bronx's rich sports history. Baseball games here are a major attraction for sports fans.

2. Bronx Zoo: One of the largest zoos in the world, the Bronx Zoo is a major destination for families and wildlife enthusiasts. It spans 265 acres and houses thousands of animals from around the globe.

3. Hip-Hop Culture: The Bronx is the birthplace of hip-hop, with pioneers like DJ Kool Herc, Grandmaster Flash, and Afrika Bambaataa originating from this borough.

The Universal Hip Hop Museum, set to open soon, will celebrate this cultural legacy.

4. Arthur Avenue: Often referred to as the "Real Little Italy," Arthur Avenue is a vibrant area known for its authentic Italian restaurants, bakeries, and markets.

Queens

Queens is the most ethnically diverse urban area in the world, offering a rich mosaic of cultures, languages, and cuisines.

1. Astoria: Known for its Greek heritage, Astoria offers a mix of cultural influences today, including Middle Eastern, South American, and Eastern European communities. The neighborhood is famous for its diverse food scene and the Museum of the Moving Image.

2. Flushing: Flushing is a bustling neighborhood with a large Asian population, particularly Chinese and Korean. Main Street is a vibrant commercial hub with numerous Asian markets, restaurants, and shops. Flushing Meadows-Corona Park, site of the 1964 World's Fair, is a major recreational area.

3. Jackson Heights: Jackson Heights is another diverse neighborhood with a significant South Asian and Latin American presence. It is known for its vibrant street life, multicultural festivals, and diverse culinary offerings.

Staten Island

Staten Island, the least populated of the five boroughs, offers a more suburban feel with extensive green spaces and historic sites.

1. Staten Island Ferry: The Staten Island Ferry provides a free, scenic commute between Staten Island and Manhattan, offering stunning views of the Statue of Liberty and the Manhattan skyline.

2. Historic Richmond Town: This living history village offers a glimpse into colonial New York, with restored homes and buildings dating back to the 17th century.

3. Greenbelt: Staten Island's Greenbelt is an extensive network of parks and natural areas, providing opportunities for hiking, birdwatching, and enjoying nature.

The neighborhoods and communities of New York City are the lifeblood of the metropolis, each contributing its own distinct flavor to the city's rich tapestry. From the cultural vibrancy of Harlem and the artistic legacy of Greenwich Village to the dynamic diversity of Queens and the historic charm of Staten Island, each area offers unique experiences and stories.

As we continue our exploration of New York, we will next delve into the city's transportation system, examining how its extensive network of subways, buses, ferries, and bridges connects its neighborhoods and supports the daily lives of millions of residents and visitors. This transportation infrastructure is not only vital for mobility but also shapes the economic and social fabric of the city.

CHAPTER 08

THE LIFELINE OF THE CITY – TRANSPORTATION INFRASTRUCTURE

New York City's transportation system is one of the most extensive and complex in the world, serving millions of residents, commuters, and tourists daily. This chapter examines the history, development, and current state of New York's transportation infrastructure, including its iconic subways, buses, ferries, and bridges.

The Subway System

1. Historical Background: The New York City Subway system, one of the oldest and largest in the world, began operation in 1904. It was initially constructed by private companies but was later consolidated under the city's control. The subway played a crucial role in shaping the city's growth and connecting its boroughs.

2. Current System: The subway system comprises 472 stations across four boroughs (Manhattan, Brooklyn, Queens,

and the Bronx) and operates 24/7. It serves over five million passengers on an average weekday, making it the lifeline of the city. Key lines include the 1/2/3 (Broadway–Seventh Avenue Line), 4/5/6 (Lexington Avenue Line), and the A/C/E (Eighth Avenue Line).

3. Challenges and Improvements: The subway system faces challenges such as aging infrastructure, overcrowding, and delays. Efforts to modernize the system include the implementation of Communication-Based Train Control (CBTC) to improve efficiency and reliability, and the introduction of new subway cars with advanced features.

Buses

1. Bus Network: The Metropolitan Transportation Authority (MTA) operates an extensive network of over 300 bus routes across the five boroughs. Buses serve areas not directly accessible by subway and provide critical connections to neighborhoods, schools, hospitals, and business districts.

2. Select Bus Service (SBS): To improve bus service efficiency, the MTA introduced Select Bus Service (SBS) routes. These routes feature dedicated bus lanes, off-board fare collection, and fewer stops, reducing travel times and enhancing service reliability.

3. Electrification and Sustainability: The MTA is working to electrify its bus fleet as part of its commitment to

sustainability. The transition to electric buses aims to reduce greenhouse gas emissions and improve air quality in the city.

Ferries

1. Staten Island Ferry: The Staten Island Ferry is a free service that operates between Staten Island and Lower Manhattan. It provides a vital connection for commuters and offers stunning views of the Statue of Liberty, Ellis Island, and the Manhattan skyline.

2. NYC Ferry: Launched in 2017, NYC Ferry is a citywide ferry service that provides additional connections between waterfront communities in Manhattan, Brooklyn, Queens, and the Bronx. The service has expanded rapidly, offering an affordable and scenic transportation option for residents and tourists.

Bridges and Tunnels

1. Iconic Bridges: New York City is home to several iconic bridges, including the Brooklyn Bridge, Manhattan Bridge, Williamsburg Bridge, and Queensboro Bridge. These bridges not only facilitate vehicular and pedestrian traffic but also serve as architectural landmarks.

2. Tunnels: The city's major tunnels include the Holland Tunnel and the Lincoln Tunnel, which connect Manhattan to New Jersey, and the Queens-Midtown Tunnel and Brooklyn-Battery Tunnel, which link Manhattan to

Queens and Brooklyn, respectively. These tunnels play a critical role in facilitating interstate and intracity travel.

3. Maintenance and Upgrades: Maintaining and upgrading the city's bridges and tunnels is a continuous effort, involving regular inspections, repairs, and modernization projects to ensure safety and efficiency.

Railroads and Airports

1. Commuter Rail: New York City is served by two major commuter rail systems: the Long Island Rail Road (LIRR) and Metro-North Railroad. These railroads connect the city to suburban areas in Long Island, the Hudson Valley, and Connecticut, providing critical links for commuters.

2. Amtrak: Amtrak's Northeast Corridor provides intercity rail service between New York City and major cities like Washington, D.C., Philadelphia, and Boston. Penn Station, the busiest rail hub in the country, serves as a central point for Amtrak and commuter rail services.

3. Airports: The city is served by three major airports: John F. Kennedy International Airport (JFK), LaGuardia Airport (LGA), and Newark Liberty International Airport (EWR). These airports handle millions of passengers annually and are critical for both domestic and international travel. Ongoing redevelopment projects aim to enhance capacity, efficiency, and passenger experience.

Bicycles and Pedestrians

1. Bike Lanes and Paths: New York City has seen a significant increase in cycling, supported by an expanding network of bike lanes and paths. The city's bike-sharing program, Citi Bike, has also grown in popularity, offering convenient and eco-friendly transportation options.

2. Pedestrian Plazas: To enhance walkability and public space, the city has created pedestrian plazas in areas like Times Square, Herald Square, and Union Square. These plazas provide safe, car-free environments for pedestrians to gather, relax, and enjoy urban life.

3. Vision Zero: Vision Zero is the city's initiative to eliminate traffic deaths and serious injuries. It involves redesigning streets, enhancing pedestrian safety measures, and enforcing traffic laws to protect all road users.

Innovations and Future Plans

1. Smart Transportation: New York City is embracing smart transportation technologies to improve mobility and reduce congestion. This includes the use of real-time data to optimize traffic flow, smart traffic signals, and intelligent transportation systems.

2. Congestion Pricing: The city plans to implement congestion pricing in Manhattan's central business district, charging vehicles a fee to enter certain areas during peak

times. This initiative aims to reduce traffic congestion, improve air quality, and generate revenue for public transportation improvements.

3. Sustainable Initiatives: The city's transportation future includes a focus on sustainability, with plans to expand electric vehicle charging infrastructure, promote alternative modes of transportation, and reduce the carbon footprint of the transportation sector.

New York City's transportation infrastructure is a vital component of its urban ecosystem, enabling the movement of people and goods across the city and beyond. From the iconic subways and bridges to the expanding bike lanes and ferry services, the city's transportation network supports its economic vitality and enhances the quality of life for its residents and visitors.

As we continue our exploration of New York, we will next delve into the city's education and healthcare systems. These essential services underpin the well-being and development of the city's population, providing education, healthcare, and social services to millions. Understanding these systems is key to appreciating the complexities and challenges of managing such a vast and diverse metropolis.

CHAPTER 09

EDUCATION AND HEALTHCARE – PILLARS OF NEW YORK CITY'S WELL-BEING

New York City's education and healthcare systems are critical to the well-being and development of its diverse population. This chapter explores the structure, challenges, and innovations within these essential services, highlighting how they contribute to the city's vitality.

Education System

New York City is home to one of the largest and most diverse public education systems in the United States. It encompasses early childhood education, K-12 schools, and higher education institutions.

1. Public Schools

- Overview: The New York City Department of Education (NYCDOE) oversees the city's public school system, serving over one million students in more than 1,800 schools. It is the largest school district in the country.

- Diversity and Inclusion: NYC schools reflect the city's multiculturalism, with students from various ethnic, linguistic, and socioeconomic backgrounds. The system offers programs for English Language Learners (ELLs), special education, and gifted and talented students.

- Challenges: The public school system faces challenges such as overcrowding, disparities in resources, and achievement gaps. Efforts to address these issues include funding reforms, targeted support for struggling schools, and initiatives to reduce class sizes.

2. Charter and Private Schools

- Charter Schools: Charter schools are publicly funded but operate independently of the traditional public school system. They offer innovative curricula and instructional approaches. Success Academy and KIPP NYC are notable examples of charter networks in the city.

- Private Schools: NYC is home to prestigious private schools, including Horace Mann, Dalton, and Trinity School. These institutions often have rigorous academic programs and extensive extracurricular offerings.

3. Higher Education

- City University of New York (CUNY): CUNY is the largest urban public university system in the United States, serving over 275,000 students across 25 campuses. It offers affordable education with a focus on accessibility and excellence.

- New York University (NYU) and Columbia University: These world-renowned private institutions contribute significantly to the city's intellectual and cultural life. NYU is known for its global reach and diverse academic programs, while Columbia is an Ivy League institution with a strong research focus.

- Community Colleges: Community colleges, such as LaGuardia Community College and Borough of Manhattan Community College, provide affordable education and vocational training, serving as crucial entry points for higher education.

4. Early Childhood Education

- Universal Pre-K: NYC offers free, full-day pre-kindergarten for all four-year-olds, known as Universal Pre-K (UPK). This program aims to ensure that children enter kindergarten ready to learn.

- 3-K for All: The city is expanding early childhood education to include three-year-olds through the 3-K for All initiative, providing early learning opportunities to more children.

5. Educational Innovations

- STEM and STEAM Programs: NYC schools emphasize STEM (Science, Technology, Engineering, and Mathematics) education, incorporating STEAM (adding Arts) to foster creativity and innovation.

- Career and Technical Education (CTE): CTE programs prepare students for careers in fields such as healthcare, information technology, and hospitality, offering pathways to employment and higher education.

Healthcare System

New York City's healthcare system is a complex network of public and private providers, ensuring access to medical care for its residents.

1. Public Health System

- NYC Health + Hospitals: The largest public health system in the country, NYC Health + Hospitals operates 11 acute care hospitals, over 70 community-based health centers, and specialized care facilities. It provides healthcare regardless of patients' ability to pay.

- Community Health Centers: Federally Qualified Health Centers (FQHCs) and other community clinics offer primary care, preventive services, and chronic disease management, particularly in underserved areas.

2. Private Hospitals and Health Systems

- Major Health Systems: New York is home to renowned private health systems, including New York-Presbyterian, Mount Sinai Health System, and NYU Langone Health. These institutions offer cutting-edge medical research, education, and patient care.

- Specialty Hospitals: The city boasts specialized hospitals like Memorial Sloan Kettering Cancer Center, Hospital for Special Surgery, and Weill Cornell Medical Center, known for their expertise in oncology, orthopedics, and other fields.

3. Public Health Initiatives

- Mental Health Services: NYC has expanded mental health services through initiatives like ThriveNYC, which aims to provide accessible mental health care and reduce stigma.

- Substance Abuse and Harm Reduction: Programs such as NYC Well and Harm Reduction Services address substance abuse issues, providing support and resources for individuals struggling with addiction.

- HealthyNYC: This initiative focuses on promoting healthy lifestyles, addressing health disparities, and improving access to healthcare across the city.

4. Healthcare Innovations

- Telemedicine: The COVID-19 pandemic accelerated the adoption of telemedicine, allowing patients to receive care remotely. NYC's healthcare providers have integrated telehealth services to enhance accessibility and convenience.

- Population Health Management: Using data and technology, healthcare providers focus on population health management to improve outcomes and reduce healthcare costs. This approach emphasizes preventive care, chronic disease management, and social determinants of health.

5. Emergency Services

- EMS and Fire Department: The Fire Department of New York (FDNY) operates the city's Emergency Medical Services (EMS), providing emergency medical care and transportation.

- Trauma Centers: Designated trauma centers across the city are equipped to handle severe injuries and emergencies, offering critical care to those in need.

6. Health Insurance and Access

- NY State of Health: The state's health insurance marketplace offers affordable coverage options through Medicaid, the Essential Plan, and Qualified Health Plans. NYC also promotes health insurance enrollment through outreach and assistance programs.

- Community-Based Organizations: Numerous organizations provide health education, enrollment assistance, and support services to ensure residents can access healthcare.

New York City's education and healthcare systems are foundational to the well-being and development of its residents. Despite facing significant challenges, these systems continue to evolve and innovate, striving to meet the diverse needs of the city's population.

As we continue our exploration of New York, we will next delve into the city's economy and industries. From Wall Street's financial powerhouses to the burgeoning tech sector, New York's economy is dynamic and multifaceted, driving growth and opportunities in one of the world's most influential cities. Understanding the economic forces at play will provide a deeper insight into the city's role on the global stage and its future trajectory.

CHAPTER 10

THE ECONOMIC ENGINE – NEW YORK CITY'S ECONOMY AND INDUSTRIES

New York City's economy is a powerhouse, driving growth and innovation not only within its borders but across the globe. This chapter explores the key industries, economic drivers, and the unique challenges and opportunities that shape the city's financial landscape.

Finance and Banking

1. Wall Street:

- Overview: Wall Street is synonymous with the financial industry, housing the New York Stock Exchange (NYSE) and NASDAQ, the world's largest stock exchanges. It is the epicenter of global finance, influencing markets worldwide.

- Major Institutions: The city is home to leading financial institutions, including Goldman Sachs, JPMorgan

Chase, Citigroup, and Morgan Stanley. These firms engage in investment banking, trading, asset management, and financial advisory services.

2. Global Financial Center:

- Foreign Investment: New York attracts significant foreign investment, serving as a hub for international banking and finance. The presence of numerous foreign banks underscores the city's global economic influence.

- Regulation and Compliance: The financial industry is heavily regulated, with institutions adhering to stringent compliance standards set by entities such as the Securities and Exchange Commission (SEC) and the Federal Reserve.

Technology and Innovation

1. Silicon Alley:

- Tech Boom: The term "Silicon Alley" refers to New York's burgeoning tech sector, centered in neighborhoods like Flatiron District and Chelsea. The city has become a major player in the tech industry, rivaling Silicon Valley.

- Key Companies: Notable tech companies with a significant presence in NYC include Google, Facebook, Amazon, and Microsoft. Startups and tech incubators like Techstars and New York City Economic Development

Corporation (NYCEDC) support innovation and entrepreneurship.

2. Fintech:

- Financial Technology: Fintech companies are transforming the financial services industry, offering innovative solutions in areas like digital payments, blockchain, and robo-advising. NYC is a leading hub for fintech startups, fostering a collaborative ecosystem.

- Investment: Venture capital investment in NYC's tech sector has surged, with billions of dollars flowing into fintech, health tech, and artificial intelligence (AI) startups.

Media and Entertainment

1. Media Giants:

- Major Players: New York is home to leading media conglomerates, including NBCUniversal, CBS Corporation, The New York Times Company, and WarnerMedia. These companies produce news, television, film, and digital content consumed worldwide.

- Publishing Industry: The city is a global center for publishing, with major publishers like Penguin Random House, HarperCollins, and Simon & Schuster headquartered here. The book publishing industry remains robust, contributing significantly to the city's economy.

2. Broadway and Theater:

- Theater District: Broadway is synonymous with world-class theater, attracting millions of visitors annually. The industry generates billions in revenue and supports thousands of jobs in production, performance, and ancillary services.

- Off-Broadway: In addition to Broadway, the city boasts a vibrant Off-Broadway and Off-Off-Broadway scene, showcasing innovative and experimental theater productions.

Real Estate and Construction

1. Skyline and Development:

- Iconic Buildings: New York City's skyline is continually evolving, with iconic skyscrapers like the Empire State Building, One World Trade Center, and new developments such as Hudson Yards reshaping the cityscape.

- Commercial Real Estate: The commercial real estate market is dynamic, with significant investments in office space, retail, and mixed-use developments. Manhattan remains a prime location for corporate headquarters and flagship stores.

2. Housing Market:

- Residential Real Estate: The city's residential real estate market is diverse, ranging from luxury condominiums to affordable housing projects. Neighborhoods like Tribeca,

SoHo, and the Upper East Side are known for their high-end properties.

- Challenges: The housing market faces challenges such as affordability, gentrification, and homelessness. Efforts to address these issues include affordable housing initiatives, rent stabilization programs, and supportive housing for vulnerable populations.

Tourism and Hospitality

1. Tourism Impact:

- Visitor Numbers: New York City is one of the most visited cities in the world, attracting over 60 million tourists annually. Key attractions include Times Square, Central Park, the Statue of Liberty, and museums such as the Metropolitan Museum of Art.

- Economic Contribution: The tourism industry contributes billions to the city's economy, supporting jobs in hospitality, retail, entertainment, and transportation.

2. Hospitality Sector:

- Hotels: The city offers a wide range of accommodations, from luxury hotels like The Plaza and The Ritz-Carlton to boutique hotels and budget options. The hotel industry is a significant driver of economic activity.

- Dining and Nightlife: New York's culinary scene is renowned globally, with diverse dining options ranging from Michelin-starred restaurants to food trucks. The nightlife industry, including bars, clubs, and live music venues, is vibrant and economically impactful.

Healthcare and Life Sciences

1. Medical Research:

- Institutions: New York is home to leading medical research institutions like Rockefeller University, Memorial Sloan Kettering Cancer Center, and NYU Langone Health. These institutions conduct cutting-edge research and clinical trials.

- Biotechnology: The city has seen growth in the biotechnology sector, with startups and research facilities focusing on drug development, genomics, and personalized medicine.

2. Healthcare Services:

- Hospitals and Clinics: NYC's healthcare system includes world-class hospitals, community health centers, and specialized clinics providing comprehensive medical care.

- Public Health: The city prioritizes public health initiatives, addressing issues such as infectious diseases, chronic conditions, and health disparities. Programs like NYC Care ensure that all residents have access to healthcare services.

Retail and Fashion

1. Fashion Capital:

- Fashion Industry: New York is a global fashion capital, hosting events like New York Fashion Week and serving as headquarters for major fashion brands and designers. The Garment District remains a key area for fashion production and innovation.

- Retail Hub: The city's retail scene is diverse, featuring flagship stores on Fifth Avenue, luxury boutiques in SoHo, and vibrant markets in neighborhoods like Williamsburg.

2. E-Commerce:

- Digital Transformation: The rise of e-commerce has transformed the retail industry, with many traditional retailers expanding their online presence. NYC-based companies like Warby Parker and Glossier have successfully integrated online and offline retail experiences.

Logistics and Transportation

1. Port Authority:

- Ports and Shipping: The Port Authority of New York and New Jersey oversees the region's major ports, facilitating international trade and logistics. The Port of New York and New Jersey is one of the busiest on the East Coast.

- Transportation Infrastructure: The Port Authority also manages critical transportation infrastructure, including airports, bridges, tunnels, and bus terminals, ensuring the efficient movement of goods and people.

2. Freight and Delivery:

- Logistics Network: The city's logistics network supports the delivery of goods to businesses and residents, with major players like UPS, FedEx, and Amazon operating extensive distribution centers and delivery fleets.

- Challenges and Innovations: The logistics industry faces challenges such as congestion, last-mile delivery, and environmental impact. Innovations like electric delivery vehicles and urban distribution centers aim to address these issues.

New York City's economy is a dynamic and multifaceted engine that drives innovation, growth, and opportunity. The city's diverse industries, from finance and technology to healthcare and hospitality, contribute to its status as a global economic leader.

As we continue our exploration of New York, we will next delve into the city's cultural and artistic heritage. From world-class museums and galleries to vibrant street art and music scenes, New York's cultural landscape is rich and varied, reflecting the creativity and diversity of its residents. Understanding the cultural fabric of the city will provide a deeper appreciation of its unique character and influence.

CHAPTER 11

CULTURE AND THE ARTS – THE SOUL OF NEW YORK CITY

New York City is a cultural powerhouse, renowned for its vibrant arts scene and rich heritage. This chapter delves into the diverse cultural and artistic expressions that make the city a global epicenter of creativity and innovation.

Museums and Galleries

1. World-Class Museums:

- The Metropolitan Museum of Art (The Met): The largest art museum in the United States, The Met houses over two million works spanning 5,000 years of history. Its collections include masterpieces from ancient Egypt, classical antiquity, and European masters.

- Museum of Modern Art (MoMA): MoMA is a leading institution dedicated to contemporary and modern art. It features works by iconic artists such as Vincent van Gogh,

Pablo Picasso, and Andy Warhol, alongside innovative temporary exhibitions.

- American Museum of Natural History: This institution is renowned for its extensive collections in natural history, including dinosaur fossils, dioramas of animal habitats, and exhibits on human evolution and space exploration.

2. Specialized Museums:

- Solomon R. Guggenheim Museum: Designed by Frank Lloyd Wright, the Guggenheim is an architectural marvel housing a prominent collection of modern and contemporary art.

- Whitney Museum of American Art: The Whitney focuses on 20th and 21st-century American art, showcasing works by Edward Hopper, Georgia O'Keeffe, and Jean-Michel Basquiat.

- The Museum of the City of New York: This museum explores the city's history and culture, offering insights into its development from a small Dutch settlement to a global metropolis.

3. Art Galleries:

- Chelsea Art District: Chelsea is home to numerous art galleries showcasing contemporary works. Prominent galleries include Gagosian, David Zwirner, and Pace Gallery.

- Lower East Side: This neighborhood is known for its experimental and emerging art scenes, with galleries like Essex Street and the New Museum driving innovation and pushing boundaries.

Performing Arts

1. Broadway and Theater:

- Broadway Theaters: Broadway is the heart of American theater, featuring world-famous productions such as "Hamilton," "The Lion King," and "Wicked." The Theater District draws millions of visitors annually, contributing significantly to the city's economy.

- Off-Broadway and Off-Off-Broadway: Beyond Broadway, New York offers a wealth of theatrical experiences in Off-Broadway and Off-Off-Broadway venues. These smaller theaters often present innovative and avant-garde productions, fostering new talent and experimental work.

2. Music and Dance:

- Carnegie Hall: A prestigious concert venue, Carnegie Hall hosts performances by leading classical musicians, orchestras, and contemporary artists from around the world.

- Lincoln Center for the Performing Arts: Lincoln Center is a cultural complex housing organizations such as the New York Philharmonic, Metropolitan Opera, and New York

City Ballet. It is a premier destination for classical music, opera, and dance.

- Jazz Scene: New York has a rich jazz heritage, with legendary clubs like The Blue Note, Village Vanguard, and Birdland offering live performances by acclaimed jazz musicians.

Literature and Publishing

1. Literary Heritage:

- Historic Figures: New York has been home to many literary giants, including Walt Whitman, F. Scott Fitzgerald, and James Baldwin. The city's literary history is celebrated in its numerous landmarks, such as the Algonquin Hotel and the New York Public Library.

- Contemporary Writers: The city continues to inspire contemporary authors, with writers like Zadie Smith, Jonathan Franzen, and Jhumpa Lahiri drawing on its rich cultural tapestry in their works.

2. Bookstores and Literary Events:

- Independent Bookstores: Independent bookstores like The Strand, McNally Jackson, and Books Are Magic are cultural hubs, hosting author readings, book signings, and literary discussions.

- Literary Festivals: Events such as the Brooklyn Book Festival and the New York City Poetry Festival celebrate the written word, bringing together authors, poets, and readers from around the world.

Visual Arts and Public Art

1. Street Art and Murals:

- Graffiti and Street Art: New York's streets are canvases for vibrant street art and graffiti. Neighborhoods like Bushwick in Brooklyn and the Lower East Side are renowned for their colorful murals and thought-provoking public art.

- Public Art Installations: The city's public spaces feature notable art installations, such as "The Vessel" at Hudson Yards and "The Charging Bull" in the Financial District. These works engage the public and enhance the urban environment.

2. Art Events and Fairs:

- The Armory Show: This annual art fair showcases contemporary and modern art from leading galleries worldwide. It attracts collectors, curators, and art enthusiasts to the city each March.

- Frieze New York: Frieze is a major art fair held on Randall's Island, featuring works from established and emerging artists. It is a key event on the international art calendar.

Film and Television

1. Film Industry:

- Iconic Filming Locations: New York City is a popular filming location for movies and television shows, with iconic landmarks and neighborhoods frequently appearing on screen. Films like "Breakfast at Tiffany's," "Taxi Driver," and "The Avengers" showcase the city's cinematic appeal.

- Film Festivals: The Tribeca Film Festival and the New York Film Festival are major events that celebrate independent filmmaking, premiering new films and hosting industry discussions.

2. Television Production:

- TV Shows: Many popular television shows are set and filmed in New York, including "Friends," "Sex and the City," and "Law & Order." The city's diverse locations and vibrant atmosphere make it a desirable setting for TV production.

- Production Studios: NYC is home to several production studios, including Silvercup Studios and Kaufman Astoria Studios, which facilitate the creation of films, TV shows, and commercials.

Cultural Diversity and Festivals

1. Cultural Celebrations:

- Parades and Festivals: New York's calendar is filled with cultural celebrations, such as the Chinese New Year

Parade in Chinatown, the West Indian Day Parade in Brooklyn, and the Puerto Rican Day Parade on Fifth Avenue. These events celebrate the city's diverse communities and heritage.

- Holiday Celebrations: Iconic holiday events like the Macy's Thanksgiving Day Parade and the Rockefeller Center Christmas Tree Lighting attract visitors from around the world, adding to the city's festive atmosphere.

2. Ethnic Enclaves:

- Neighborhoods: New York's neighborhoods reflect its multiculturalism, with areas like Little Italy, Harlem, and Jackson Heights offering rich cultural experiences, including authentic cuisine, music, and traditions.

New York City's cultural and artistic landscape is a vibrant mosaic that reflects its diverse population and rich history. The city's museums, theaters, galleries, and cultural institutions are integral to its identity, fostering creativity and innovation.

As we continue our exploration of New York, the next chapter will delve into the city's infrastructure and transportation systems. Understanding the complexities and innovations within these sectors will provide a comprehensive view of how the city operates and sustains its dynamic pace of life. From the iconic subway system to the intricate network of bridges and tunnels, the infrastructure is the backbone of New York City's functionality and growth.

CHAPTER 12

INFRASTRUCTURE AND TRANSPORTATION – THE BACKBONE OF NEW YORK CITY

New York City's infrastructure and transportation systems are the lifeblood of its daily operations, supporting the flow of people, goods, and services across the metropolis. This chapter explores the complexities and innovations within these sectors, shedding light on how the city sustains its dynamic pace of life.

Public Transportation

1. Subway System:

- Overview: The New York City Subway, operated by the Metropolitan Transportation Authority (MTA), is one of the world's largest and busiest rapid transit systems. With 472 stations across four boroughs, it serves millions of riders daily.

- History and Development: The subway opened in 1904 and has since expanded significantly. Its history is marked by periods of growth, decline, and revitalization, reflecting the city's broader economic and social trends.

- Challenges and Improvements: The system faces challenges such as aging infrastructure, overcrowding, and delays. Recent initiatives like the Subway Action Plan aim to address these issues through increased funding, modernization efforts, and improved maintenance practices.

2. Buses:

- MTA Bus Network: The MTA also operates an extensive bus network, covering areas not served by the subway. Buses play a crucial role in connecting neighborhoods and providing accessibility to all city residents.

- Select Bus Service (SBS): SBS routes offer faster and more efficient service with features like dedicated bus lanes, off-board fare collection, and fewer stops. These routes are designed to reduce travel times and enhance the overall transit experience.

3. Commuter Rail:

- Long Island Rail Road (LIRR): The LIRR is the busiest commuter railroad in North America, connecting Manhattan to Long Island. It serves as a vital link for suburban commuters and contributes to regional economic integration.

- Metro-North Railroad: Metro-North operates commuter rail services between New York City and its northern suburbs, including Westchester County, Connecticut, and beyond. It is essential for connecting the city to its broader metropolitan area.

Roadways and Bridges

1. Major Highways:

- Interstate System: Major highways like I-95, I-87, and I-278 traverse the city, facilitating interstate travel and regional connectivity. These routes are vital for the movement of goods and long-distance travel.

- Parkways and Expressways: New York City is also served by an intricate network of parkways and expressways, including the Grand Central Parkway, the Brooklyn-Queens Expressway (BQE), and the FDR Drive, which help manage intra-city traffic.

2. Iconic Bridges and Tunnels:

- Brooklyn Bridge: An iconic symbol of New York, the Brooklyn Bridge connects Manhattan and Brooklyn over the East River. Opened in 1883, it is renowned for its architectural beauty and historical significance.

- George Washington Bridge: This double-decked suspension bridge spans the Hudson River, linking Manhattan to New Jersey. It is one of the busiest bridges in the world, handling both vehicular and pedestrian traffic.

- Holland and Lincoln Tunnels: These tunnels connect Manhattan with New Jersey, facilitating significant daily commuter and freight traffic under the Hudson River.

Airports and Seaports

1. Airports:

- John F. Kennedy International Airport (JFK): JFK is one of the busiest international airports in the United States, serving as a major gateway for international travel. It offers extensive flight connections and advanced facilities.

- LaGuardia Airport (LGA): LGA primarily handles domestic flights and is known for its proximity to Manhattan. Recent renovations have modernized its terminals and improved passenger experience.

- Newark Liberty International Airport (EWR): Located in New Jersey, EWR serves the New York metropolitan area, providing both domestic and international flights. It is a critical hub for transcontinental and global travel.

2. Seaports:

- Port of New York and New Jersey: This port is one of the busiest on the East Coast, handling a significant volume of cargo traffic. It plays a crucial role in international trade and logistics, supporting the regional economy.

- Cruise Terminals: The city is a major cruise destination, with terminals like the Manhattan Cruise Terminal and the Brooklyn Cruise Terminal serving as departure points for cruises to the Caribbean, Europe, and beyond.

Innovative Transportation Solutions

1. Biking and Bike Sharing:

- Citi Bike: The Citi Bike program offers a bike-sharing service with thousands of bicycles available at docking stations across the city. It promotes sustainable transportation and provides an affordable alternative for short trips.

- Bike Lanes: The city has invested in expanding its network of bike lanes and cycling infrastructure, encouraging more residents to use bicycles for commuting and recreation.

2. Ride-Sharing and Taxis:

- Yellow Cabs: The iconic yellow taxi remains a ubiquitous mode of transport in New York City. Regulated by the Taxi and Limousine Commission (TLC), these cabs provide reliable and accessible service across the city.

- Ride-Sharing Services: Companies like Uber and Lyft have transformed the transportation landscape, offering flexible and convenient ride-hailing options. These services complement traditional taxis and public transit, catering to diverse travel needs.

3. Pedestrian Initiatives:

- Plaza Program: The NYC Department of Transportation's Plaza Program transforms underused streets into vibrant public spaces, enhancing pedestrian safety and community engagement. Notable examples include Times Square and the Union Square pedestrian plaza.

- Vision Zero: Launched in 2014, Vision Zero aims to eliminate traffic fatalities and serious injuries. The initiative focuses on improving street design, enforcing traffic laws, and raising public awareness to create safer streets for all users.

Urban Planning and Development

1. Sustainable Development:

- Green Building Initiatives: New York City has adopted green building standards, promoting energy efficiency and sustainability in new developments. Programs like LEED certification encourage the construction of environmentally friendly buildings.

- Resilient Infrastructure: In response to climate change and extreme weather events, the city is investing in resilient infrastructure. Projects include coastal protection, stormwater management, and the elevation of critical facilities.

2. Smart City Innovations:

- Technology Integration: New York is leveraging technology to enhance urban living, with initiatives like LinkNYC providing free public Wi-Fi and smart kiosks offering information and services.

- Data-Driven Decision Making: The city uses data analytics to improve urban planning and service delivery. Programs like NYC Analytics aggregate data from various sources to inform policy decisions and optimize resource allocation.

Public Utilities and Essential Services

1. Water Supply and Management:

- New York City's Water Supply: The city's water supply system is one of the most sophisticated in the world, delivering high-quality drinking water from upstate reservoirs through a vast network of aqueducts and tunnels.

- Wastewater Treatment: The city's wastewater treatment facilities ensure that sewage is treated and discharged safely, protecting water quality and public health.

2. Electricity and Energy:

- Energy Grid: Con Edison operates the city's electric grid, providing reliable power to millions of residents and businesses. The grid is continually upgraded to meet increasing demand and enhance resilience.

- Renewable Energy: New York is investing in renewable energy sources, including solar and wind power, to reduce its carbon footprint and promote sustainability. Programs like the New York State Energy Research and Development Authority (NYSERDA) support these initiatives.

New York City's infrastructure and transportation systems are essential to its functionality and growth, supporting the daily lives of millions of residents and visitors. From the extensive subway network to the iconic bridges and cutting-edge urban innovations, these systems are the backbone of the city's dynamic and ever-evolving landscape.

As we continue our exploration of New York, the next chapter will focus on the city's educational institutions and intellectual heritage. From prestigious universities to renowned research centers, New York's commitment to education and knowledge has made it a global hub for learning and innovation. Understanding the city's educational landscape will provide insights into the intellectual vitality that fuels its progress and success.

CHAPTER 13

EDUCATION AND INTELLECTUAL HERITAGE – THE MIND OF NEW YORK CITY

New York City is a global hub for education and intellectual pursuits, boasting a diverse array of prestigious institutions, innovative programs, and vibrant academic communities. This chapter delves into the city's rich educational landscape, highlighting its universities, research centers, public schools, and cultural contributions to intellectual life.

Universities and Colleges

1. Ivy League and Prestigious Institutions:

- Columbia University: An Ivy League institution founded in 1754, Columbia University is renowned for its rigorous academic programs, world-class faculty, and influential alumni. It is a leading research university with a strong emphasis on humanities, sciences, and professional studies.

- New York University (NYU): NYU is one of the largest private universities in the United States, known for its diverse academic offerings and urban campus in Greenwich Village. It excels in fields such as law, business, arts, and social sciences.

- The City University of New York (CUNY): CUNY is the largest urban public university system in the country, comprising 25 institutions, including senior colleges, community colleges, and graduate schools. It provides accessible education to a diverse student body and plays a vital role in the city's educational landscape.

2. Specialized Institutions:

- The Juilliard School: Located at Lincoln Center, Juilliard is a world-renowned performing arts conservatory, offering programs in music, dance, and drama. Its alumni include many prominent artists and performers.

- Fashion Institute of Technology (FIT): FIT is a leader in fashion, design, and related fields, providing specialized education that combines creativity with practical skills. Its programs are highly regarded in the fashion industry.

- Pratt Institute: Based in Brooklyn, Pratt is a prestigious art and design school offering programs in architecture, fine arts, and industrial design. It is known for fostering innovation and creativity.

Research and Innovation

1. Research Universities and Centers:

- Rockefeller University: A world-leading biomedical research institution, Rockefeller University focuses on basic and clinical research in the life sciences. Its faculty includes many Nobel laureates and groundbreaking scientists.

- Weill Cornell Medicine: Part of Cornell University, Weill Cornell Medicine is a premier medical school and research center, contributing to advancements in medical science and healthcare.

- New York Genome Center: This collaborative research facility focuses on genomic research and its applications in medicine. It brings together scientists from various institutions to address complex biological questions.

2. Innovation and Technology:

- Cornell Tech: Situated on Roosevelt Island, Cornell Tech is a graduate school that integrates technology, business, law, and design. It aims to foster innovation and entrepreneurship through interdisciplinary collaboration.

- New York City's Tech Ecosystem: The city is home to a thriving tech ecosystem, with numerous startups, incubators, and accelerators. Institutions like NYU Tandon

School of Engineering and Columbia's Data Science Institute play key roles in driving technological advancements.

Public Education

1. New York City Department of Education:

- Public Schools: The NYC Department of Education oversees the largest public school system in the United States, serving over a million students across more than 1,800 schools. The system includes elementary, middle, and high schools, as well as specialized and charter schools.

- Specialized High Schools: NYC is known for its specialized high schools, such as Stuyvesant High School, Bronx High School of Science, and Brooklyn Technical High School. These schools offer rigorous academic programs and attract top-performing students.

2. Educational Programs and Initiatives:

- Universal Pre-K: New York City offers universal pre-kindergarten programs, providing early childhood education to all four-year-olds. This initiative aims to promote equity and prepare children for academic success.

- Community Schools: The city has implemented community schools that provide comprehensive support services to students and families, addressing academic, social, and health needs.

Cultural and Intellectual Contributions

1. Libraries and Archives:

- The New York Public Library (NYPL): NYPL is one of the largest public library systems in the world, with 92 locations across the city. Its main branch, the Stephen A. Schwarzman Building, is a historic landmark and a treasure trove of books, manuscripts, and special collections.

- Morgan Library & Museum: Originally the private library of financier J.P. Morgan, this museum and research library houses rare books, manuscripts, and artworks. It offers a rich cultural experience for scholars and the public.

2. Intellectual Communities:

- Think Tanks and Research Institutes: New York City is home to numerous think tanks and research institutes, such as the Council on Foreign Relations and the Brookings Institution. These organizations contribute to policy discussions and intellectual discourse on global and domestic issues.

- Literary Societies and Clubs: The city boasts a vibrant literary scene, with institutions like the National Arts Club and the New York Society Library hosting readings, lectures, and literary events.

Adult Education and Lifelong Learning

1. Continuing Education Programs:

- New School for Social Research: Known for its progressive approach, the New School offers continuing education programs in social sciences, humanities, and arts. It provides opportunities for lifelong learning and professional development.

- School of Professional Studies (NYU SPS): NYU SPS offers a wide range of continuing education programs, including certificates, workshops, and courses in various fields. It caters to working professionals seeking to enhance their skills and knowledge.

2. Community Colleges and Adult Education Centers:

- Borough of Manhattan Community College (BMCC): BMCC, part of the CUNY system, offers associate degree programs and continuing education opportunities. It serves a diverse student population and provides pathways to higher education and career advancement.

- Adult Learning Centers: The city operates adult learning centers that offer GED preparation, literacy programs, and vocational training. These centers support adult learners in achieving their educational and career goals.

New York City's educational institutions and intellectual heritage are integral to its identity as a global center of learning and innovation. From prestigious universities to vibrant public schools, and from cutting-edge research centers to community learning programs, the city's commitment to education and intellectual pursuits drives its progress and success.

As we continue our exploration of New York, the next chapter will focus on the city's economic landscape and business environment. We'll examine the key industries, financial markets, and entrepreneurial spirit that fuel New York's economy, making it one of the most influential and dynamic cities in the world. Understanding the economic forces at play will provide a comprehensive view of how New York thrives as a global economic powerhouse.

CHAPTER 14

THE ECONOMIC LANDSCAPE – NEW YORK CITY'S FINANCIAL POWERHOUSE

New York City is a global economic giant, with an economy that influences markets worldwide. Its dynamic business environment, leading financial institutions, and diverse industries contribute to its status as a major financial hub. This chapter explores the economic landscape of New York City, highlighting key sectors, market activities, and the entrepreneurial spirit that drives its economy.

Financial Markets and Institutions

1. Wall Street:

- Overview: Wall Street is synonymous with New York City's financial power. Located in the Financial District of Lower Manhattan, it is home to the New York Stock Exchange (NYSE), the largest stock exchange in the world by market capitalization.

- NYSE: The NYSE, founded in 1792, is a central hub for global finance, where stocks of major corporations are traded. It plays a critical role in capital formation, economic growth, and market stability.

- NASDAQ: Another key player is the NASDAQ, known for its high-tech listings and electronic trading platform. It has revolutionized trading practices and is a significant force in the technology sector.

2. Investment Banks and Financial Services:

- Major Firms: New York City hosts the headquarters of major investment banks like Goldman Sachs, JPMorgan Chase, Morgan Stanley, and Citigroup. These institutions provide a wide range of financial services, including investment banking, asset management, and wealth management.

- Hedge Funds and Private Equity: The city is also a hub for hedge funds and private equity firms, which manage substantial assets and influence financial markets globally.

Key Industries

1. Real Estate:

- Commercial Real Estate: New York City's skyline is defined by its iconic skyscrapers and office buildings. The commercial real estate sector is vital to the city's economy, with major developments like Hudson Yards and One World Trade Center setting new benchmarks.

   - Residential Real Estate: The residential market is equally important, with diverse housing options ranging from luxury apartments in Manhattan to brownstones in Brooklyn. The city's real estate market is dynamic, reflecting changing demographics and economic conditions.

   2. Media and Entertainment:

   - Television and Film: New York City is a major center for television and film production. Studios like Silvercup and Kaufman Astoria, along with networks such as NBC, ABC, and CBS, contribute to a thriving media industry.

   - Publishing: The city is a global publishing powerhouse, home to major book publishers, magazines, and newspapers, including The New York Times, HarperCollins, and Penguin Random House.

   3. Technology and Innovation:

   - Silicon Alley: Known as Silicon Alley, New York's tech sector is rapidly growing, with startups and established companies in areas like fintech, digital media, and e-commerce. The city's tech ecosystem is supported by incubators, accelerators, and venture capital firms.

   - Biotech and Health Tech: New York City is also making strides in biotech and health tech, with institutions like the Alexandria Center for Life Science fostering innovation in medical research and technology.

4. Tourism and Hospitality:

- Tourist Attractions: New York City is one of the world's top tourist destinations, attracting millions of visitors each year. Iconic landmarks like Times Square, Central Park, and the Statue of Liberty draw tourists from around the globe.

- Hotels and Restaurants: The city's hospitality industry is extensive, with a wide range of hotels, restaurants, and entertainment venues. Culinary diversity and world-class dining experiences make New York a gastronomic capital.

5. Fashion and Retail:

- Fashion Industry: As a global fashion capital, New York hosts major events like New York Fashion Week and is home to top designers, fashion houses, and showrooms. The Garment District remains a vital part of the industry.

- Retail Sector: The city boasts a vibrant retail scene, from luxury boutiques on Fifth Avenue to eclectic shops in SoHo. Major department stores like Macy's and Bloomingdale's are iconic shopping destinations.

Entrepreneurship and Small Businesses

1. Startup Ecosystem:

- Incubators and Accelerators: Programs like Techstars, Y Combinator, and New York City Economic

Development Corporation (NYCEDC) initiatives support startups through funding, mentorship, and resources.

- Coworking Spaces: Coworking spaces such as WeWork, Knotel, and The Wing provide flexible office solutions and foster collaborative communities for entrepreneurs and small businesses.

2. Small Business Support:

- NYC Small Business Services (SBS): SBS offers various programs and services to support small businesses, including access to capital, business courses, and assistance with permits and regulations.

- Business Improvement Districts (BIDs): BIDs play a crucial role in revitalizing commercial areas, improving infrastructure, and supporting local businesses through collective efforts and funding.

Economic Development and Policies

1. Incentives and Programs:

- Tax Incentives: New York City provides various tax incentives to attract businesses and stimulate economic growth. These include credits for job creation, real estate development, and research and development activities.

- Economic Zones: Designated economic zones, such as the Lower Manhattan Development Zone and the

Brooklyn Navy Yard, offer additional incentives and resources to encourage investment and development.

2. Sustainable Development:

- Green Initiatives: The city promotes sustainable development through initiatives like PlaNYC and OneNYC, which focus on reducing greenhouse gas emissions, improving energy efficiency, and enhancing urban resilience.

- Public-Private Partnerships: Collaborative efforts between the public and private sectors drive many development projects, leveraging resources and expertise to achieve economic and social goals.

Challenges and Future Outlook

1. Economic Inequality:

- Income Disparities: Despite its wealth, New York City faces significant income inequality. Addressing disparities through equitable policies and inclusive economic growth remains a priority.

- Affordable Housing: The high cost of living and housing affordability are pressing issues. Initiatives to increase affordable housing and support low-income residents are essential for sustaining the city's diverse population.

2. Economic Diversification:

- Diversifying Industries: To ensure long-term economic stability, New York is focusing on diversifying its economic base. Expanding sectors like technology, healthcare, and green energy are part of this strategy.

- Workforce Development: Investing in education and workforce development is crucial for preparing residents for future job markets. Programs that provide training and skills development are key to maintaining a competitive workforce.

New York City's economic landscape is a testament to its resilience, adaptability, and innovative spirit. From the bustling financial markets of Wall Street to the vibrant startup ecosystem, the city continues to be a beacon of economic opportunity and growth. Its diverse industries, robust infrastructure, and strategic initiatives position it as a global economic powerhouse.

As we approach the final chapter of our exploration of New York, we will turn our attention to the city's cultural and social fabric. We'll delve into the arts, community life, and the unique character that makes New York a vibrant and inclusive metropolis. Understanding these aspects will complete our comprehensive view of the city and its enduring allure.

CHAPTER 15

THE CULTURAL AND SOCIAL FABRIC – THE SOUL OF NEW YORK CITY

New York City's vibrant cultural and social life is as dynamic and diverse as its population. The city is a melting pot of cultures, ideas, and artistic expressions, which come together to create a unique and electrifying atmosphere. This chapter explores the various facets of New York's cultural and social fabric, highlighting its arts, community life, and the distinctive character that makes the city an unparalleled urban experience.

The Arts

1. Visual Arts:

- Museums: New York City is home to some of the world's most renowned museums. The Metropolitan Museum of Art, the Museum of Modern Art (MoMA), the Whitney Museum of American Art, and the Solomon R. Guggenheim

Museum are just a few that attract millions of visitors each year.

- Galleries: The city's art galleries, particularly in Chelsea and the Lower East Side, showcase contemporary art and emerging artists. These galleries play a crucial role in the global art market and cultural discourse.

2. Performing Arts:

- Theater: Broadway is synonymous with world-class theater. With its storied history and array of musicals and plays, Broadway remains a pinnacle of performing arts. Off-Broadway and Off-Off-Broadway theaters also contribute significantly to the city's theater scene, offering innovative and experimental performances.

- Dance: New York is a major center for dance, hosting companies such as the New York City Ballet, the American Ballet Theatre, and the Alvin Ailey American Dance Theater. These institutions perform at venues like Lincoln Center and the Joyce Theater.

- Music: The city's music scene is diverse, encompassing everything from classical performances at Carnegie Hall to cutting-edge jazz at the Blue Note and underground hip-hop in Brooklyn. The New York Philharmonic and the Metropolitan Opera are pillars of classical music.

3. Literature and Writing:

- Bookstores: Independent bookstores like The Strand and McNally Jackson are cultural hubs for book lovers. They host readings, signings, and literary events that foster a vibrant literary community.

- Literary Events: Events such as the Brooklyn Book Festival and the PEN World Voices Festival celebrate literature and provide platforms for authors to engage with readers.

Community Life

1. Neighborhoods:

- Diversity: New York City's neighborhoods are a tapestry of cultural diversity. Areas like Chinatown, Little Italy, Harlem, and Jackson Heights are renowned for their unique cultural identities and vibrant communities.

- Gentrification and Change: Neighborhoods continually evolve due to factors like gentrification. While this can bring economic growth and development, it also raises concerns about displacement and cultural preservation.

2. Festivals and Parades:

- Cultural Festivals: The city hosts numerous cultural festivals that celebrate its diverse heritage. The Puerto Rican Day Parade, the West Indian American Day Carnival, and the Lunar New Year Parade are just a few examples.

- Pride and Inclusivity: New York City is known for its inclusivity and celebration of LGBTQ+ rights. The annual NYC Pride March is a vibrant and significant event that attracts participants and spectators from around the world.

3. Social Movements and Activism:

- Historical Movements: The city has a rich history of social movements, including the Harlem Renaissance, the Stonewall Riots, and the Occupy Wall Street movement. These movements have shaped not only the city but also national and global conversations on civil rights and social justice.

- Contemporary Activism: Today, New York City continues to be a hub for activism. Organizations and community groups work tirelessly on issues such as racial equality, climate change, and economic justice.

Culinary Scene

1. Restaurants and Dining:

- Diverse Cuisine: The city's culinary scene reflects its cultural diversity. From Michelin-starred restaurants to food trucks, New York offers a gastronomic journey through global cuisines. Neighborhoods like Flushing for Chinese food, Astoria for Greek cuisine, and the East Village for Japanese izakayas showcase this diversity.

- Street Food: Food carts and trucks are an integral part of the city's food culture. Iconic foods like hot dogs, pretzels, and halal carts are ubiquitous, providing quick and delicious options for locals and visitors alike.

2. Markets and Festivals:

- Farmers' Markets: Markets such as the Union Square Greenmarket offer fresh, locally sourced produce and artisanal goods, fostering a connection between urban residents and regional farmers.

- Food Festivals: Events like the New York City Wine & Food Festival and Smorgasburg celebrate culinary innovation and provide opportunities to sample diverse dishes.

Sports and Recreation

1. Professional Sports:

- Teams: New York City is home to iconic sports teams like the New York Yankees (MLB), the New York Knicks (NBA), the New York Giants (NFL), and the New York Rangers (NHL). These teams have passionate fan bases and storied histories.

- Venues: Venues such as Yankee Stadium, Madison Square Garden, and Citi Field are not just sports arenas but cultural landmarks that host a variety of events beyond sports.

2. Recreational Activities:

- Parks and Green Spaces: Central Park, Prospect Park, and the High Line offer residents and visitors spaces for recreation, relaxation, and community activities. These parks are essential to the city's quality of life.

- Fitness and Wellness: New Yorkers have access to a wide range of fitness and wellness options, from yoga studios and gyms to cycling paths and outdoor fitness classes.

New York City's cultural and social fabric is a mosaic of artistic expression, community life, culinary delights, and recreational opportunities. Its vibrant neighborhoods, diverse communities, and rich cultural heritage make it a city like no other. The arts thrive in its museums, theaters, and music halls; communities celebrate their heritage through festivals and parades; and the culinary scene offers a taste of the world in every bite.

As we conclude this volume, it is clear that New York City's essence lies in its ability to blend tradition with innovation, fostering a dynamic environment where diversity and creativity flourish. This exploration of the city's various facets reveals a metropolis that is constantly evolving, yet deeply rooted in its rich history and cultural diversity.

The final chapter will reflect on the themes explored throughout this volume and consider what the future holds for New York City. We will examine the challenges and opportunities that lie ahead, and how this extraordinary city can continue to inspire and lead on the global stage.

www.ingramcontent.com/pod-product-compliance
Lightning Source LLC
Chambersburg PA
CBHW061322120726
48001CB00002B/637